BBQ

COOKING

Recipes from the private collection of
John Farris

Cover and Illustrations by
Kenneth Crouse

Designed and Edited by

L.E.B. Inc.
27599 Schoolcraft
Livonia, Michigan 48150

Come to a Barbecue!

In this book, I hope to share some of my favorite outdoor cooking techniques and recipes with those who enjoy preparing complete meals on a barbecue grill. All of the recipes, which have been tested in a number of barbecue cooking classes, serve between 4-8. They can be easily altered to serve larger or smaller groups, so call your friends and neighbors, gather your family, plan your meal and say: *"Come to a barbecue!"*

John Farris

Barbecue Equipment

Kettle type grills: I enjoy using a kettle-type grill. I generally build my fire on one side of the pit and cook on the other side with the hood on to prevent heat loss. If the wind is blowing from the west, I close the vents on the bottom and place the fire on the side of the grill facing west. When I am finished cooking, I close all vents, shutting off the air and forcing the fire to go out. The charcoal can be used again. I prefer this type of grill, and use charcoal for my cooking because I can build the fire as I desire, and more accurately regulate the heat. If there aren't any adjustments on the bottom or top of the kettle, make sure the coals are elevated from the bottom.

Charcoal: I prefer a good hardwood briquet over the inexpensive brands. No matter what kind of charcoal used, **do not** allow carcinogens to come in contact with your food by cooking directly over the coals. This allows melted fat to hit the hot coals and the rising smoke and fumes are hazardous. In this book, I emphasize cooking over a foil pan containing water to catch the grease. I also use the term 'indirect" which means the same thing. Delicious charcoal flavor can be maintained using these techniques.

Gas Grills: Propane gas is a good cooking medium, and gas grills are gaining in popularity. Regulating the temperature is a little tricky because the heat source is closer to the food. For safety, I advise observing the same precautions as with the charcoal grill.

*A **homemade grill for special purposes:*** A 55 gallon drum cut in half makes an excellent grill for large groups. The top half, with hinge and handle attached, is the cover. Place one inch of gravel in the bottom to prevent bottom of drum from burning out. Install a wire rack to elevate the coals, and another across the top to hold the food. Drill four 1/2 inch holes around bottom half, and three 1 inch holes within a 4 inch circle in the top to allow air flow. If building a frame for this type of grill, do not use galvanized steel; it gives off a dangerous gas when heated. The bed of coals does not need to be deep; after coals are started and gray, spread them out. A base of 2 briquets thick is enough. Most people use more charcoal than is necessary.

Setting the fire: The food you are grilling determines the kind of fire to set. Foods that cook quickly such as steaks, chops, hot dogs and kabobs require a hot fire. To make a **hot** fire, mound briquets 5-6 deep, soak with lighter fluid five minutes prior to lighting, make and place a foil pan next to coals then light fire at the base of the mound. Leave cover off until fire dies down, with tongs adjust coals to desired depth for cooking, and adjust foil pan to desired area. Then put on cover with vents fully open. Let coals burn 15-20 minutes, or until gray before cooking is started. With tongs, adjust coals to just two deep for a **medium** fire; to decrease the heat further for a **slow** fire, partially close grill vents. Heat the grill grate before putting on meat. Tap the top of the grill with tongs to knock ashes off the coals. When grilling is completed, close all vents and put the hood on tightly; this will snuff out the fire, and the coals can be reused.

Over the Coals

Beef
John's Steak Broiling Tips
John's Rotisserie Roasting Tips

Pork & Lamb
John's Pork Barbecue tips

"Try Lamb!"
Fish and Fowl
John's Fish Barbecue Tips

John's Poultry Barbecue Tips

Sauces & Marinades

Desserts

BEEF

BEEF

John's Steak Broiling Tips:

-Choose tender steaks, about 1 inch thick.

-Trim outer edge of fat and slash fat at edges to keep steaks flat.

-When coals are hot, tap off gray ash with fire tongs.

-Heat grill top, grease it and put on steaks; orders for rare go on last.

-Heat forces the juices to the uncooked surface, so when you see bubbles on the top of meat, steaks are ready to turn.

-Turn steaks with tongs and pancake turner, not fork, to preserve juices.

-Turn only once, and broil second side for shorter time than first.

-For medium rare, allow 13-15 minutes total broiling time.

-Salt and pepper each browned side <u>after turning</u>, or as you remove them from the grill. Serve sputtering hot.

-For a crusty, char-flavored coating, sear one side by lowering grill top close to coals for 2-3 minutes, then raise grill to complete cooking.

-To carve a big steak, cut close to bone and remove it; cut across full width of steak in 1 inch slices, narrowing a little on the tenderloin side to be sure everyone gets a section of choice meat. Slice tail section last for seconds.

John's Rotisserie Roasting Tips:

-Choose a large roast, 3 1/2-4 pounds so it will still be juicy when cooked.

-Have butcher tie roast at 1 inch intervals to make it compact; if very lean, have outside covered with a layer of fat before tying.

-Chuck roasts and arm roasts are very good for barbecuing. When meat is done, separate the muscles and carve across the grain to insure good flavor and tenderness.

-To insert pieces of garlic into a roast, push the tip of a knife into the meat and insert a piece of garlic as the knife is withdrawn. Pull the meat together over the slit.

-Insert spit through center of roast so that it is evenly balanced. Insert meat thermometer into center of roast into heaviest part of meat, not touching bone, fat, or spit.

-Arrange hot coals at back of firebox, a drip pan in front of coals and under roast. The coals don't need to be as hot as for broiling. Knock off gray ash, attach spit and turn on motor.

-Cook until meat thermometer reads 140° for rare, 160° for medium and 170° for well-done. Most roasts will cook a little faster than in an oven. A boneless roast will need to cook longer than a bone-in roast, such as standing rib.

-When meat is done, let it 'firm' 15-20 minutes before carving. Can just lower firebox and let it rotate for that time, or remove to a platter.

1 CRACKED PEPPER STEAK

Not too peppery, just right!

4 lbs chuck steak, 2 1/2 - 3 inches thick
instant seasoned meat tenderizer
3 T cracked or coarsely ground pepper

Slash fat edges of steak. Sprinkle all surfaces of steak with tenderizer, using about 1/2 teaspoon per pound of meat. <u>Do not salt.</u> To insure penetration, pierce all sides deeply every 1/2 inch with a long-tined fork and work tenderizer in. Press pepper into both sides of steak.

Place steak on grill about 3 inches from coals and broil for 35-50 minutes, turning frequently with tongs and a turner. To serve, slice thinly with sharp knife across grain of meat at about a 30° angle. Serves 6-8.

Beef

2 ROTISSERIE ROUND

3 lbs eye-of-round steak, 2 1/2-3 inches thick
instant non-seasoned meat tenderizer
1 C catsup
1/3 C Worcestershire sauce
1 C water
1 t chili powder
1 t salt
1 clove garlic, minced

Sprinkle all sides of steak evenly with tenderizer, using 1/2
teaspoon per pound. <u>Do not salt</u>. Pierce all sides of steak
every 1/2 inch with a long-tined fork. Combine remaining
ingredients and simmer for 30 minutes.

Center steak on motorized spit and tie with cord. Roast
slowly over coals for 1 1/2 hours, or until done as desired,
basting frequently with sauce. Serves 8.

3 MARINATED HICKORY STEAKS

The difference between steak and roast is the thickness and price.

2, 2 lb round-bone arm roasts, 1 inch thick
10 small cloves garlic, peeled
seasoned salt
pepper
1/2 C oil
1/2 C wine vinegar
1 T Worcestershire sauce

Insert tip of sharp knife in meat and insert garlic cloves as you withdraw knife, using five cloves garlic for each steak. Sprinkle meat generously with seasonings. Combine oil, vinegar and Worcestershire sauce; pour over steaks in a shallow dish and marinate for several hours at room temperature, turning occasionally. Broil over hot coals with hickory, about 15 minutes per side, basting frequently with marinade. Remove garlic before serving. Heat remaining marinade and serve with steak. Serves 8.

Beef

4 CHATEAUBRIAND

A classic recipe with new elegance

1 beef tenderloin, 2 - 2 1/2 lbs
1, 4 oz pkg blue cheese
1 T brandy

Cut off the narrow tail of the tenderloin to use for *Tender-loin Medallions.* Trim fat from surface of meat. Make a slanting cut, 2 inches deep, the full length of the meat with a sharp, narrow-bladed knife held at a 45° angle. Turn meat and make another cut on other side. Blend cheese and brandy; spread cheese mixture in the openings formed by the cuts. Skewer slashes closed with short skewers. Tie meat with string at both ends and in middle. Balance on spit and rotate over <u>hot</u> coals 1 1/4 - 1 1/2 hours for medium rare. Serves 6-8.

5   TENDERLOIN MEDALLIONS

A good appetizer

1/2 lb thinly sliced tip of beef tenderloin
1/2 C orange juice
1/4 C brandy
2 T drawn butter

Cut sliced tenderloin in 1x3 inch strips; weave onto bamboo or metal skewers. To make drawn butter, heat butter and pour off the clear, yellow liquid that comes to the top. Use only the clear liquid in this recipe. (Remaining sediment may be used in sauces.) Combine orange juice and brandy with drawn butter and baste meat as it grills. Serves 4.

Beef

6 MARINATED BEEF CUBES

Cooked in a foil pan without fat

1/2 C salad oil
1/4 C vinegar
1/4 C chopped onion
1 t salt
1 t coarsely ground pepper
2 t Worcestershire or steak sauce
2 lbs lean beef, round or chuck

Cut meat in 1 1/2 inch cubes. Combine marinade ingredients, add meat and mix well. Refrigerate overnight, or let stand at room temperature 2-4 hours, turning occasionally. Drain marinade, leaving onion with meat. Cook in a foil pan over medium coals until done as desired. Serves 6.

7   CAMP STEW

A Boy Scout favorite

2 lbs beef stew meat
1 1/2 C water
1 8 oz can tomato sauce
2 t salt
1/4 t pepper
1 t Worcestershire sauce

2 bay leaves
2 onions, quartered
6 carrots, quartered
4 potatoes, quartered
2 C lima beans, drained
1 C whole kernel corn

Brown meat in a small amount of fat in a heavy Dutch oven. Add water, tomato sauce, onions and seasonings. Place hot coals around covered pan and simmer for about 1 1/4 hours. Add carrots and potatoes and cook for 30 minutes; add corn and beans and heat through. If desired, thicken with 2 tablespoons flour blended with 1/4 cup water. Serves 8.

Beef

8 APPETIZER MEAT BALLS

These behave, the egg keeps them intact

1/2 lb ground beef
1 egg
1 t flour
2 t grated onion
3/4 t salt
1/4 t pepper

Combine ingredients and shape into 1 inch balls. Broil
over hot coals in a foil pan that has been punctured hit and
miss. Toss damp hickory chips on coals if you like a
smoky flavor. Serve on toothpicks. 24 meatballs.

9 BURGUNDY BEEFBURGERS

Deliciously flavored with butter and wine

2 lbs ground chuck
1 C soft bread crumbs
1 egg
1/4 C Burgundy wine
2 T sliced green onions
salt and pepper

Sauce:
2 T sliced green onions
1/2 C butter
1/4 C Burgundy wine
6 slices French bread

Mix ground chuck, bread crumbs, egg, 1/4 cup wine,
onions, salt and pepper; shape mixture into 6 doughnut
shaped burgers about 1 inch thick. Cook remaining onions
in 1/2 cup butter and add wine. Broil burgers over coals
about four inches from heat for 9 minutes, brushing frequently with sauce. Turn burgers and broil 4 minutes,
again basting with sauce. Serve on thick, diagonally-sliced
French bread.   Heat remaining sauce to pass. Serves 6.

Beef

10 STUFFED HAMBURGERS

Butter-browned mushrooms between meat patties

2 lbs ground beef
3 eggs
1 1/2 T flour
1 medium onion, grated
1 T salt
1/4 t pepper

2 C raw mushrooms
1/4 C butter
8 slices bacon

Mix beef, eggs, flour, onion, salt and pepper; roll mixture into a thin sheet and cut into 16 patties with a large cookie cutter or water glass. Saute mushrooms in butter and spread over 8 of the patties. Place remaining patties on top and pinch edges. Wrap a slice of bacon around edge of each burger and tack with a toothpick. Broil over coals, with hood of grill down for about 4 minutes on each side. Serves 8.

11 BEEF KABOBS WITH FLAIR

3 lbs lean beef, round or chuck
1 lb fresh mushrooms
cherry tomatoes
pineapple chunks
green pepper squares
onion wedges

Marinade:
1 C salad oil
3/4 C soy sauce
1/2 C lemon juice
1/4 C Worcestershire sauce
1/4 C prepared mustard
1 T cracked pepper
2 cloves garlic, minced

Combine marinade ingredients. Cut meat in 1 1/2 inch cubes and add to marinade; cover and refrigerate for 24-36 hours, turning meat occasionally. Fill skewers, alternating meat with mushroom caps. Broil over hot coals to rare or medium rare, brushing frequently with melted butter or margarine, and turning often. Serves 6-8.

Beef

12 MARINATED BEEF TIPS

Appetizer for eight or main dish for two

1 lb beef tips
2 T diced onion
1 T brown sugar
1/2 C Burgundy wine

Combine onion, brown sugar and wine; marinate beef tips
in mixture for at least 1 hour. Place on small skewers and
grill.

13 ISLAND TERIYAKI

1/2 C soy sauce
1/4 C brown sugar
2 T olive oil
1 T grated ginger root
  or 1 t dried ginger

1/4 T coarsely ground pepper
2 cloves garlic, minced
1/2 t MSG
1 1/2 lbs top sirloin steak
canned water chestnuts

Mix all ingredients except meat. Cut meat in strips 1/4 inch thick, and about 1 inch wide. Add meat to marinade and let stand at room temperature for 2 hours. Lace meat accordion style on skewers, putting a chestnut on end. Broil over hot coals 10-12 minutes, turning often and basting with marinade. Serves 4-5.

Beef

14 ROLLED RIB ROAST

5-6 lb rolled rib roast
3 cloves garlic
1/4-1/3 C horseradish

Crush two garlic cloves and combine with horseradish;
spread mixture on roast before it is rolled, or unroll meat,
spread with mixture, reroll and tie securely. Balance roast
on spit. Rub outside surface with a cut clove of garlic and
brush with horseradish, using some of the liquid. Insert
meat thermometer. Refer to *John's Rotisserie Roasting
Tips* to complete cooking. Three servings per pound.

15 CAMPFIRE POT ROAST
Serve with *Quick Bordelaise Sauce**

4 lbs blade pot roast, 1 1/2 inches thick
salt and pepper
1/2 stalk celery, sliced on diagonal
6 small whole carrots
1 medium green pepper, cut in rings
2 medium onions, quartered
2 medium tomatoes, cut in wedges

Brown roast for 15 minutes on greased grill over hot coals
with damp hickory added. Season well with salt and
pepper. Tear off a 5 foot length of aluminum foil and fold
double. Place meat in center of foil and cover with
vegetables. Fold foil and seal securely. Bake without
turning over slow coals 1 1/2 -2 hours or until tender. Use
drippings in sauce. Serves 6-8.

* See *Sauces and Marinades*

Beef

16 DIXIE POT ROAST

4 lbs pot roast, 1 1/2 inches thick
 salt and pepper
2 stalks celery, sliced on diagonal
2 carrots, sliced
1/2 t dry mustard
1 medium onion, sliced
3/4 C catsup
3 T flour
1 T Worcestershire sauce
1 T brown sugar
1 T vinegar

Brown roast for 20-30 minutes over hot coals with hickory
added. Season with salt and pepper. Combine all other
ingredients for sauce. Tear a 5 foot length of foil and fold
double. Spoon half of sauce on foil; place meat on sauce,
cover with vegetables and remaining sauce. Seal foil and
place on grill covered with a double layer of foil. Bake
roast over slow coals 1 1/2 -2 hours or until tender.
Serves 6-8.

John's Pork Barbecue Tips

-Spareribs are rib bones from the bacon strip. Consult your butcher and purchase extra-meaty loin back ribs which are tops for barbecuing. Plan on 3/4 lb per serving.

-Perfect ribs are crispy and brown on the outside, tender and juicy inside and should show no pink when cut. Long, slow cooking with frequent turning is required. To tenderize and cut grilling time in half, bake and steam ribs in oven by placing ribs in a pan on top oven shelf with a pan of water below. Bake for 35-40 minutes at 375°.

-Internal temperature for pork **must** be at 165° or higher to be done and safe to serve.

-Enjoy grilling pork without the risk of carcinogens caused by greasy smoke rising from the hot coals. When grilling pork ribs or any fatty meat, build the fire on one side of the grill and cook on the other side. Make a foil pan and place it next to the coals. Put water in the pan to catch drippings.

-Pork doesn't need to be basted.

17   RIBS WITH RODEO SAUCE

For honest, cookout flavor? You can't beat these

4 lbs pork spareribs
1 lemon, thinly sliced
1 large onion, thinly sliced
Sauce:
1 C catsup
1 T Worcestershire sauce

2-3 dashes hot pepper sauce
1 C water
1/2 C vinegar
1 T sugar
1 t salt
1 t celery seed

Combine sauce ingredients and simmer for 30 minutes.
Salt ribs and place on rack over slow coals. *Follow John's
Pork Barbecue Tips.* Put grill hood down and cook 1 hour
without turning. Brush ribs with sauce and fasten slices of
lemon and onion to ribs with toothpicks. Continue cooking
without turning for 30-40 minutes or until done, brushing
now and then with sauce. For smoke flavor, toss damp
hickory chips or sawdust over coals during last half hour.
Snip ribs into serving pieces with scissors. 4 servings.

Pork

18 HICKORY SMOKED SPARERIBS

4 lbs loin back ribs
1 recipe *West Side Barbecue sauce* *
1/2 lemon, thinly sliced
1/2 large onion, thinly sliced

Salt ribs and place bone side down on barbecue. *Follow John's Pork Barbecue Tips.* Add dampened hickory to slow coals and close hood. Cook for 3 1/2 hours without turning. For last half hour, baste with sauce and peg slices of lemon and onion onto meat with toothpicks. Serves 4.

* See *Sauces and Marinades*

19   BARBECUED SPARERIBS

4 lbs spareribs
1 medium onion, sliced
1 lemon, thinly sliced
Sauce:
2 T butter or margarine
2 cloves garlic, crushed
2 T prepared mustard
1/4 C brown sugar

1 C catsup
3/4 C chili sauce
1 T celery seed
2 T Worcestershire sauce
1-2 dashes hot pepper sauce
1/2 t salt
1 1/2 C water

Saute garlic in butter 4-5 minutes; blend in mustard and sugar. Add remaining sauce ingredients and bring to a boil. Set aside. Salt ribs and place bone side down on grill over slow coals. *Follow John's Pork Barbecue Tips.* Broil for about 20 minutes. Turn and brown other side. Turn again and broil 20 minutes. Brush meaty side with sauce and fasten lemon and onion slices on with toothpicks. Broil without turning 20-30 minutes more, or until done, basting occasionally. To finish, brush on sauce and broil 2-3 minutes on each side. Serves 4.

Pork

20   RIBS AND KRAUT

Tender and juicy with a new twist

tart apples, cored and cut in 1/2 inch rings
sauerkraut
caraway seed
loin back ribs, in 3 rib sections

For each serving, fold a 36 inch length of foil in half. Just
off-center, place 2 apple rings, 1/2 C sauerkraut, *(do not
rinse kraut)* a sprinkle of caraway seed and two, 3 rib
sections of ribs, or desired amount for the serving. Sprinkle
with salt and pepper, fold and seal foil and cook over
glowing coals 1 hour, or until meat is well done.

21   BARBECUED PORK BACKS

The pineapple-chili glaze is absolutely delicious!

3 lbs meaty pork backbones, or spareribs
1 C chili sauce
1 C pineapple preserves
1/3 C vinegar

Sprinkle meat with salt and broil with bone side down over
slow coals for 20 minutes. Turn and brown other side.
Turn again and broil 20 minutes. Combine glaze ingredients and brush on meat; continue broiling without turning
until done, basting occasionally. To finish, baste both sides
and broil 3-4 minutes per side. 6-8 servings.

22   CHINESE SMOKED RIBS

A nice blend of flavors

6 lbs loin back or spare ribs
Barbecue seasoning:
2 T sugar
1/2 t salt
1/4 t each: paprika, MSG
    turmeric, celery seed,
    and dry mustard

Ginger sauce:
1/2 C soy sauce
1/2 C catsup
1/4 C water
3 T brown sugar
2 T grated ginger root or
   2 t ground ginger
1 t MSG

Mix ginger sauce ingredients and let stand overnight.
Combine ingredients for barbecue seasoning and rub on
ribs; let stand 2 hours. Brush ribs with sauce and let stand
for 1 hour. Cook according to *John's Pork Barbecue Tips,*
1 1/2 hours for spareribs, or 2 hours for loin ribs, brushing
occasionally with sauce. Serves 6-8.

23 BACON WRAPPED CHESTNUTS

A great combination

1 lb bacon
1 can whole waterchestnuts

Partially cook bacon and drain to remove grease. Cut bacon slices in half. Open and drain chestnuts. Place one chestnut on one end of bacon strip and roll up. Secure with a toothpick. Place on pierced piece of foil on grill top. Broil until golden brown. 8 servings of 4 pieces each.

24 Bacon Wrapped Mushrooms

Another great combination

Follow directions for *Bacon Wrapped Chestnuts*, using fresh mushrooms about 1 1/2 inch in diameter, or cut larger mushrooms in half. Wipe mushrooms with a damp cloth before wrapping in bacon.

25 PORK ROAST ON A SPIT

The incomparable flavor of hickory

4-5 lb pork loin roast
Marinade:
1 1/2 C salad oil
3/4 C soy sauce
1/4 C Worcestershire sauce
2 T dry mustard

2 1/4 t salt
1 T coarsely ground pepper
1/2 C wine vinegar
1 1/2 t parsley flakes
2 cloves garlic, crushed
1/3 C lemon juice

Have butcher split bone between each rib of roast. Combine marinade ingredients and marinate meat 1-2 days in refrigerator, turning occasionally.* Balance meat on spit over drip pan, in front of coals topped with damp hickory chips. Turn on motor and roast about 2 1/2 hours or until meat thermometer reads 170°, basting occasionally with marinade. (Do not undercook.) Halfway through cooking, add more hickory chips; when they start to blaze, pick them up with tongs, extinguish blaze in water and return chips to coals. The smoke makes the hickory flavor.

Marinade can be reused; store tightly and freeze, or refrigerate for 1 week.

23 BACON WRAPPED CHESTNUTS

A great combination

1 lb bacon
1 can whole waterchestnuts

Partially cook bacon and drain to remove grease. Cut
bacon slices in half. Open and drain chestnuts. Place one
chestnut on one end of bacon strip and roll up. Secure with
a toothpick. Place on pierced piece of foil on grill top.
Broil until golden brown. 8 servings of 4 pieces each.

24 Bacon Wrapped Mushrooms

Another great combination

Follow directions for *Bacon Wrapped Chestnuts*, using
fresh mushrooms about 1 1/2 inch in diameter, or cut larger
mushrooms in half. Wipe mushrooms with a damp cloth
before wrapping in bacon.

Pork

25   PORK ROAST ON A SPIT

The incomparable flavor of hickory

4-5 lb pork loin roast	2 1/4 t salt
Marinade:	1 T coarsely ground pepper
1 1/2 C salad oil	1/2 C wine vinegar
3/4 C soy sauce	1 1/2 t parsley flakes
1/4 C Worcestershire sauce	2 cloves garlic, crushed
2 T dry mustard	1/3 C lemon juice

Have butcher split bone between each rib of roast. Combine marinade ingredients and marinate meat 1-2 days in refrigerator, turning occasionally.* Balance meat on spit over drip pan, in front of coals topped with damp hickory chips. Turn on motor and roast about 2 1/2 hours or until meat thermometer reads 170°, basting occasionally with marinade. (Do not undercook.) Halfway through cooking, add more hickory chips; when they start to blaze, pick them up with tongs, extinguish blaze in water and return chips to coals. The smoke makes the hickory flavor.

Marinade can be reused; store tightly and freeze, or refrigerate for 1 week.

26 BROILED PORK TENDERLOIN

Pork like you've never tasted before

1 pork tenderloin, sliced 1 inch thick on the diagonal
2 T butter
1/4 t hot pepper sauce
salt and pepper

Place steaks on a greased grill; broil over hot coals until browned on both sides and no longer pink in center, about 12-15 minutes. Combine butter and pepper sauce and brush on both sides of meat. Salt and pepper just before removing to a warmed serving platter. 2 servings.

Pork

27 ROAST BONELESS PORK LOIN

Serve with your favorite barbecue sauce

4-5 lb boneless pork loin	2 T coriander
1 1/2 C brown sugar	1/2 t cayenne pepper
2 T black pepper	1 t mace
1 t fennel seed	

Mix brown sugar and spices. Trim most of fat and cut loin in half; place one half, fat side down on cutting board. Place all seasoning on top of meat and cover with other half of loin, fat side up. Tie the two pieces together with cord. Place loin on grill, away from medium coals with a foil pan beneath to catch drippings. Allow 1 1/2-2 hours for roast to reach necessary internal temperature. *See John's Pork Tips.* Remove from grill and let stand at room temperature 10-15 minutes to prevent loss of juices when meat is sliced. Slice and serve with a favorite barbecue sauce. Serves 8.

28 HAWAIIAN HAM ON A STICK

Ham lusciously glazed and pineapple caramelized

3 lbs fully cooked ham
1 fresh pineapple
melted butter
1 C brown sugar
1/2 C honey
1/2 C orange juice

Cut ham into 1 1/2 inch cubes. Cut pineapple into cubes.
Alternate ham and pineapple on skewers. Combine sugar,
honey and juice. Place skewers on grill and brush kabobs
with butter and honey mixture until hot and glazed. Turn
often. Serves 6-8.

Pork

29   SASSY FRANKS

1 lb frankfurters (8-10)
1/4 C chopped celery
1/4 C chopped green pepper
1/4 C butter or margarine
1 can tomato soup
1/4 C brown sugar

1/4 C water
3 T vinegar
1 T Worcestershire sauce
1/4 t garlic salt
1/2 lemon, thinly sliced
1/2 onion, thinly sliced

Cook celery and pepper in butter until almost tender; add remaining ingredients except franks, onion and lemon and simmer uncovered for 15 minutes. Score franks in criss-cross fashion and grill over hot coals. Add lemon and onion slices to sauce and simmer again for 15 minutes. Drop grilled franks in sauce. Serve on buns with sauce. Serves 4-5.

30   BARBECUED BOLOGNA

1, 3 to 4 lb *big* bologna, unsliced
1 C catsup
1/3 C butter, melted
1 1/2 T Worcestershire sauce
1 1/2 T brown prepared mustard
1 1/2 t onion salt

Score bologna with 1/4 inch deep diagonal lines. Anchor
meat on spit, and place a drip pan below meat. Cook with
hood down over medium coals for 1 1/4 hours or until
heated through and nicely browned. Combine remaining
ingredients for sauce and brush on meat during last 15
minutes of cooking. Slice 1/4 inch thick and serve on
toasted hamburg buns; spoon on remaining sauce.
8 servings.

Pork

31 ROAST SUCKLING PIG

Plan a party and serve this delightful feast of pork

1 12-14 lb suckling pig
salt and pepper
sage or fruit stuffing
soft butter

Clean pig, rinse cavity, scrub outside with a stiff brush and pat dry. Season cavity with salt and pepper and stuff loosely with a sage or fruit dressing. Lace cavity closed tightly with string. Truss by bringing the feet forward and tying them with string in a kneeling position. Place a ball of foil in the mouth and cover the nose, ears and tail with foil to prevent over-browning. Brush all exposed skin with soft butter. Insert a meat thermometer into the thigh, not touching spit, bone or fat.

Use a covered grill with a cooking surface at least 24 inches long. Place hot coals at back of firebox and place a foil pan the length of the pig in front of coals. Place the pig on a spit or place directly on the grill and lower hood. Adjust damper so that meat will cook slowly. If cooked on grill top, you may need to cover the side facing the coals with foil to prevent it from browning too quickly. Cook 2-2 1/2 hours, or until thermometer reaches 170°, basting occasionally with pan drippings. When meat is done, arrange it on a plank, remove foil from head and tail and replace foil ball in mouth with an apple. Traditionally, the suckling pig is decorated with a necklace of raw cranberries and two cranberries for eyes.

To carve: Carve through the thigh joint first as you would a turkey, removing the hams and legs first. Cut these pieces in slices. Next, start in the center of the pig and cut right down through the ribs. Serve two little ribs, a portion of stuffing and a slice from the hams to each person. Serves 10-12.

Pork

"Try Lamb. You'll like it!"

Lamb, the "new" red meat has become more popular in the last few years, for many reasons besides great taste when barbecued or roasted in the oven.

-Lamb is the only table meat that is unaffected by antibiotics and hormones because it goes to market so young. Most American lamb is no more than 6 months old when it goes to market, and is superior to imported lamb because of the way it is bred and raised.

-American lamb is naturally lean because of its age and therefore has less fat and marbling than beef. It is lower in calories than either beef or poultry. A three ounce serving from the loin or leg contains only 176 calories.

Lamb

32   BROILED LAMB CHOPS

Have rib, loin or shoulder chops cut 3/4 - 1 inch thick. Cut
fat in several places around edges of chops to prevent
curling, or broil in a wire broiler basket. Rub hot grill or
broiler basket with fat from chops or bacon to prevent
sticking. Arrange chops on grill indirectly over hot coals.
When brown on one side, sprinkle with seasoned salt and
turn. Allow 12-15 minutes for chops one inch thick.

33   LAMB CHOPS WITH PARMESAN
Ask the butcher to "french" rib chops for you

6 lamb chops about 3/4 inch thick
1/4 C Parmesan cheese
2 T soft butter
salt and pepper

Broil chops 5-6 inches from medium coals for 6-8 minutes.
Turn and broil 4-5 minutes more or until done as desired.
Blend remaining ingredients and spread on chops. Broil for
1-2 minutes more. Serves 6.

Lamb

34 AMERICAN SHISH KABOB

A traditional Near East marinade,
also wonderful on poultry

2 lbs boneless lamb
green peppers, quartered
red peppers, quartered
thick onion slices
1/2 C olive oil
1/4 C lemon juice
1 t salt

1 t marjoram
1 t thyme
1/2 t pepper
1 clove garlic, minced
1/2 C chopped onion
1/2 C snipped parsley

Combine ingredients for marinade. Cut lamb in 1 1/2 inch
cubes and put meat in marinade, mixing well. Refrigerate
overnight or let stand at room temperature for 2-3 hours,
turning occasionally. Fill skewers, alternating meat with
green and red peppers and onion slices. Broil over hot
coals, turning frequently until medium rare. Brush with
melted butter while broiling. Serves 6.

35 MARINATED LAMB SQUARES

Don't skewer these squares

2 envelopes garlic salad dressing mix
2/3 C chopped onion
3/4 C chopped celery tips and leaves
1/3 C vinegar
1/2 C salad oil
1/2 C cooking sherry
1 T Worcestershire sauce
2 lbs boneless lamb

Cut lamb into 1 1/2 inch cubes. Combine all other ingredients and add meat, stirring to coat. Refrigerate overnight or let stand at room temperature 2-3 hours, turning occasionally. Transfer meat and marinade to a foil pan and place pan over hot coals. Brown meat and continue cooking until medium done, (a bit pink on the inside). Do not overcook. Discard marinade and serve meat hot with rice. Serves 6.

36 ROTISSERIE LEG OF LAMB

4-5 lb leg of lamb
5 cloves fresh garlic
seasoning salt
2 C black coffee

Have the butcher bone and tie, or "jet-net" the leg of lamb.
Peel garlic and cut each clove into 2-4 strips. With a sharp
knife, cut slits 1/2 inch deep all around the leg and insert a
strip of garlic into each one, then pull the openings shut.
Sprinkle with seasoning salt and place meat on rotisserie
skewer. Build fire so that coals will be on two sides of
roast. Prepare a foil pan and set it between the coals, and
fill pan with water. Before starting roast, coals should be
gray. Place grill hood down and allow 2 - 21/2 hours
roasting time, basting occasionally with black coffee.
After 1 1/2 hours, check internal temperature with a meat
thermometer. Roast will be done when temperatue reaches
140°. Remove from grill, remove skewer and let meat rest
10 - 15 minutes before slicing to prevent loss of juices.
Slice thinly and serve. Serves 8.

37 BUTTERFLY LEG OF LAMB

Lamb with a butterfly shape

1 leg of lamb, 5-6 lbs
1/2 C salad oil
1/2 C lemon juice
1/4 C grated onion
1/2 C cooking sherry

1-2 cloves garlic, minced
1 t thyme
1 t salt
1/2 t selected herbs

Have butcher bone lamb and slit it lengthwise to spread it flat like a thick steak. Combine marinade ingredients in a large flat glass dish. Place meat in marinade and let stand one hour at room temperature or overnight in the refrigerator, turning occasionally. Drain and save marinade. Insert 2 long skewers through meat forming an X, or place meat in a broiler basket to keep it from curling during cooking. Roast over medium coals 1 1/2 - 2 hours, or until medium done, turning every 15 minutes. Baste frequently with reserved marinade. Remove to carving board and carve across grain into thin slices. 8 servings.

Lamb

FISH & FOWL

John's Fish Tips

The few basic rules for cooking fish and seafood are easy
to follow, even though each kind of fish has individual
flavor, texture and appearance.

- Allow 6-8 ounces of dressed fish per serving

*-If you make allowances for fat content of fish, you can
successfully use almost any cooking method for almost
any fish.* For example, fish with high fat content can be
broiled without basting, and lean fish may be broiled if you
baste with melted butter to prevent drying.

-Avoid over cooking. Fish should be moist and tender with
delicate flavor. Fish is done when it flakes apart easily
when touched with a fork.

-Don't over-handle fish during cooking and serving.
Cooked fish breaks apart easily, so turn only once during
cooking, use a broiler basket, and serve on a warm platter.

-Never leave fresh fish soaking in water. This causes
loss of flavor and makes the flesh flabby. Wash fish
quickly, drain and dry on paper toweling.

38 GRILLED TROUT ALMONDINE

Can also cook each fish in buttered foil

4 brook trout, 8 oz each	1/2 C butter
1/4 C flour	2 T slivered almonds
1/2 t salt	1/4 C lemon juice
dash pepper	2 T snipped parsley

Clean and remove heads from fish; wash and pat dry with paper towels. Combine flour, salt and pepper; dip fish in seasoned flour and place in an oiled wire broiler basket or wrap individually in buttered foil, leaving plenty of space for air expansion. Broil fish over hot coals, basting with 1/4 C melted butter, if using a basket. Cook for 15 minutes or until fish flakes easily, turning once during cooking. Brown almonds in remaining butter and add lemon juice and parsley. Pour sauce over grilled fish on a serving platter. Serves 4.

Fish

39 CHARCOALED TROUT STEAKS

Careful not to over cook; when flesh flakes, its done

6 lake trout, northern trout, or muskies
1/3 C melted butter
1 1/2 T lemon juice
salt and pepper

Brush fish with butter and place in an oiled wire broiler
basket. Broil indirectly over hot coals 2 inches from heat
for 5 minutes. Turn, brush with lemon butter and broil five
minutes more until fish flakes. Season with salt and
pepper. Serves 6.

40 CAMPFIRE FISH FRY

One pound fish makes two servings

1/3 C yellow corn meal	2 T flour
1 t salt	1/4 t paprika
1 lb fish fillets	1/4 C oil

Combine dry ingredients and dip fish in mixture to coat.
Heat oil in skillet over hot coals for 10 minutes. Fry fillets

until brown on one side, about 4 minutes. Turn and brown other side, cooking until fish flakes easily. Thin fillets cook quickly. Do not over cook. Fry small fish whole; bone and fillet larger fish.

41 SPEEDY BROILED FISH

Soy sauce lends a surprise tingle

1 lb halibut or other fish	2 T oil
salt and pepper	2 T lemon juice
2 t soy sauce	2 T snipped parsley

Cut fillets in serving size pieces; season with salt and pepper. Combine soy sauce and oil. Arrange fish on an oiled grill, in an oiled wire broiler basket, or if fish tends to be dry, on oiled foil that has been slit at intervals. Broil until fish is golden brown, about 5-8 minutes on each side, basting frequently with oil mixture. Remove to a warm platter. Heat remaining oil, add lemon and parsley and pour mixture over fish. Serves 4.

42   MARINATED SALMON STEAKS

Wine marinade keeps fish moist while broiling

4 salmon steaks, 3/4 inch	3/4 C dry white wine
salt and pepper	1/4 C lemon juice
2 T butter or margarine	salt and pepper
	1/2 t dry mustard

Combine wine, lemon juice, salt, pepper and mustard.
Marinate salmon steaks (or halibut) in mixture for 1 hour.
Drain and reserve marinade. Sprinkle steaks with salt and
pepper and broil over hot coals for 5 minutes on one side.
Turn and brush with butter. Broil 5-7 minutes longer, or
until fish flakes. Brush both sides with butter and remove
to warm platter. Brush lightly with remaining marinade.
Serves 4.

43 HALIBUT HEAVEN

Remember this recipe for a spectacular dinner!

2 lb fresh or frozen halibut   1/2 C dairy sour cream
2 T soy sauce   3/4 C fine corn flake crumbs
1 t lemon juice   1/2 C toasted sesame seed
salt and pepper

Thaw fish until fillets come apart. Brush pieces with
mixture of soy sauce and lemon juice, season with salt and
pepper. Coat both sides with sour cream and roll in
mixture of crumbs and seeds. Place coated fillets in an
oiled wire broiler basket. Broil over medium coals about
10 minutes, turning once. Serves 4.

Fish

44 SHRIMP-OUT

1 lb raw shrimp
1/2 C soda crackers, crushed
1 egg, slightly beaten
1/3 C salad oil
1/2 flour

Sauce Diablo:
1/2 C chili sauce
1-2 t Tobasco
1-2 T horseradish
1 T lemon juice

Peel and devein shrimp; roll in flour, dip in egg, drain, and coat well with cracker crumbs. Let pieces stand in oil for 1 minute and drain slightly on paper toweling. Cook on wire screen indirectly over hot coals, 5-8 minutes or until shrimp are done and crumbs browned. Serve with *Sauce Diablo.* Serves 4.

45 SAUCY SHRIMP

Shrimp cocktail with "cooked-out" character

1 lb large shrimp, peeled and deveined
Marinade:
1 C *Westside Barbecue Sauce**
3 T lemon juice
1 T Worcestershire sauce
1 t dill weed

Combine marinade ingredients and pour over shrimp; cover
and let stand 6-12 hours in refrigerator, stirring occasionally. Cook shrimp on a fine wire grill over hot coals,
turning once and brushing often with marinade. Cook for
6-8 minutes or until done. Do not over cook. Heat remaining marinade and serve with shrimp. Serves 4.

* See *Sauces and Marinades*

46   SHRIMP KABOBS WITH NOODLES

Marinade is also sauce for the noodles!

46-50 cooked shrimp
54 green and ripe olives
54 cherry tomatoes
1 12 oz pkg wide noodles
1 T Dry Vermouth
1/2 t dried mint leaves

Marinade:
1 C salad oil
1 C lemon juice
1 T garlic salt
2 t paprika
1 t seasoned salt

Blend marinade ingredients and pour over shrimp; refrigerate for 2 hours. Drain, reserving marinade. Alternate shrimp, olives and tomatoes on skewers; brush with marinade. Broil 4 inches from heat, 2 minutes on each side, turning and basting once. Cook noodles in salted water. Add vermouth to marinade and toss mixture with noodles and mint. Serves 8.

Kabob tip: set up an assembly line. Lay the skewers in a row and thread the first ingredient on each one; repeat with each ingredient until skewers are filled.

47 SEAFOOD KABOBS

Cut green pepper ovals to prevent burned corners

4 king crab legs, 3 1/2 lbs unshelled
5 medium onions
4 medium tomatoes, quartered
4 medium green peppers
1/4 C lemon juice
1/4 C melted butter

Remove raw crabmeat from cracked shells and cut in 2 inch
pieces. Peel and quarter onions, removing center core to
make pieces "cup-shaped." Slice each side of green pepper
into an oval. (Use the leftovers for salad.) On four 12 inch
skewers, string pieces of onion, crab, tomato and green
pepper. Combine butter and lemon juice and brush over
filled skewers. Broil about 3 inches from heat for 7 minutes. Turn, brush with sauce and broil for 7 more minutes.
Pass drawn butter and lemon wedges. Serves 4.

Fish

48 SCALLOPS 'N BACON

Bacon and scallop flavors blend over charcoal fire

1 lb fresh or frozen scallops
1/4 C butter or margarine, melted
2 T lemon juice
1/2 t salt
dash white pepper
sliced bacon
paprika

Thaw frozen scallops; wash, removing any shell particles.
Combine butter, lemon juice, salt and pepper. Pour mixture
over scallops and let stand for 30 minutes, turning once.
Drain. Cook bacon in a skillet until it begins to ruffle, but
is still flexible. Drain on paper towels and cool. Wrap
each scallop in 1/2 slice bacon, sprinkle with paprika and
secure with a toothpick. Place scallops on foil and broil
indirectly over medium hot coals for five minutes. Turn,
sprinkle with paprika and broil second side 5 - 7 minutes,
or until bacon is crisp and brown. Serves 4.

49 BARBECUED ROCK LOBSTER TAILS

4 medium Rock lobster tails
1/4 C butter or margarine, melted
2 t lemon juice
1 t grated orange peel
1/4 t each: ground ginger, aromatic bitters,
          and chili powder

Thaw lobster tails and cut off thin undershell membrane
with kitchen shears. Bend tail back to crack shell or insert
long skewers lengthwise between shell and meat to prevent
curling. Combine melted butter with lemon, orange peel
and spices; brush over lobster. Broil on grill over hot coals
for about 5 minutes with meat side up. Turn shell side up,
brush with sauce and continue to broil 5-10 minutes until
meat is no longer transparent, but opaque. Serve
immediately. Serves 4.

**To broil lobster tails in kitchen range broiler: Prepare as
above and place shell side up on broiler pan. Broil for
about 5 minutes, turn, brush with sauce and continue to
broil 5-10 minutes.

Johns Poultry Barbecue Tips

-Grill chicken on foil with holes pierced in it rather than directly over the coals.

-Chicken may be cooked from start to finish on the grill. Place pieces on grill skin side down, and season top side. Wait until about 10 minutes before chicken is done before adding barbecue sauce to avoid burning chicken on the outside before it is done on inside.

-To reduce grilling time by half, pre-cook chicken before grilling. Add 1 carrot, 2 ribs celery, 1/2 onion and 2 whole cloves to 3 quarts of water. Bring mixture to a boil and simmer 10 minutes. Add whole chicken or pieces of chicken to pot and simmer 15-20 minutes. Cool for 10 minutes before placing on grill. (Reserve broth for chicken soup.)

-You can bake a 10-12 pound turkey right on the coals in about 1 1/2-2 hours. Wrap bird in 12 layers of foil and place it directly on gray coals. Turn only once, about 3/4 hour into cooking time.

50 PATIO CHICKEN BARBECUE

Not too tangy a sauce

2 split broilers, 2 - 2 1/2 lbs each
Sauce:
1 C tomato sauce
1/2 C water
1/4 C molasses
2 T butter
1 T Worcestershire sauce

2 T minced onion
2 T vinegar
2 t dry mustard
1 t salt
1/4 t pepper
1/4 t chili powder

Combine sauce ingredients and simmer 15-20 minutes. Brush chicken with salad oil and sprinkle with salt and pepper; place on grill over slow coals, bone side down, and grill 25 minutes. Turn and broil for 20 minutes. Brush with sauce and continue broiling, turning occasionally and basting with sauce for 10-15 minutes or until chicken is tender. 4 servings.

Poultry

51 Honey Mustard Chicken

Quick and easy; can also be broiled in oven

4 chicken broiler halves
olive oil
1/2 C honey
3 T soy sauce
juice of two lemons
3 garlic cloves, chopped
2 t prepared mustard

Brush chicken with oil and broil over medium coals until
about half done. Combine remaining ingredients and brush
chicken with honey mixture, brushing and turning every
5 minutes until chicken is done, keeping fire fairly slow.
Serves 4.

52 Marinated Drumsticks

For kids of all ages

12 chicken drumsticks
1/4 C catsup
2-3 T lemon juice
2 T soy sauce
1/4 C cooking oil

Combine all ingredients except chicken, mixing well. Add
chicken legs and turn to coat with marinade. Refrigerate
overnight, turning occasionally. Place drumsticks in a
broiler basket and broil over medium coals, turning occasionally and basting with marinade. Broil about 1 hour or
until tender. Serves 6.

53 ORIENTAL CHICKEN BREASTS

Broil in the oven if grilling is out of season

4 boned and skinned chicken breasts
1/3 C white wine
1 1/2 t Worcestershire sauce
1/2 t ground ginger
salt and pepper
paprika

Combine wine, Worcestershire sauce and ginger in a bowl.
Place chicken in mixture and turn to coat; refrigerate for
2 hours before cooking. Grill chicken 5 minutes on each
side or until done as desired. Season with salt and pepper.
Place chicken on platter; sprinkle with paprika for color
and garnish with parsley. Serves 4.

54 CHICKEN NICOISE

Chicken and rice with delicious tomato sauce

4 boneless chicken breasts
1/2 C lemon juice
1/2 C Worcestershire sauce
1/4 t Tabasco sauce
Sauce:
1/2 C diced onion
1/8 t garlic salt

6 fresh tomatoes
1/2 C chicken stock
1/8 t sugar
1/4 t chili powder
1/4 C scallions bias-cut
1/2 C Monterey Jack cheese,
    shredded

Mix lemon juice, Worcestershire and Tabasco; marinate
chicken in mixture for 24 hours. Saute half of onion and
garlic in small amount of butter. Puree 4 tomatoes, remaining onion, chicken stock, sugar and chili powder; pour
mixture into sauted onion, and simmer for 5 minutes. Dice
remaining tomato and add to sauce with scallions; simmer
again for 5 minutes. Grill or broil chicken 5 minutes on
each side or until done. Prepare rice. Place each chicken
breast on bed of rice, ladle sauce over chicken and top with
cheese. Serves 4.

Poultry

55   SWISS ALMOND CHICKEN

Chicken wrapped in dried beef. Simply delicious

4 chicken breast halves
4 slices dried beef
Sauce:
1/4 C margarine
3 C sliced fresh mushrooms
1/4 C chopped onion
3 T flour
1/8 t black pepper

1/8 t marjoram leaves
1/8 t thyme
1 C milk
1 1/2 C Swiss cheese
1/3 C cooking sherry
1/2 C slivered almonds
1/3 C bacon bits

Saute mushrooms and onions in margarine; stir in flour, pepper and herbs. Gradually add milk and cook, stirring constantly until thickened. Remove from heat and stir in shredded Swiss cheese and sherry.

Skin and debone chicken. Wrap one slice dried beef around each breast; place pieces in a sprayed foil pan over medium coals. Cook 10-15 minutes; cover with sauce and bake with grill cover down for about 1 hour. Garnish with almonds and bacon bits. Serves 4.

56 CURRIED CHICKEN

Orange-glazed with cilantro

4 chicken breasts, deboned	1 1/2 T curry powder
1 T diced garlic	1 1/2 t cumin
3 T butter	1 1/2 t basil
2/3 C orange juice	1 t chopped parsley
1/2 C chicken stock	1 T prepared mustard
1 T grated orange rind	1/2 t each salt and pepper
4 T chopped fresh cilantro	2 T cornstarch

Pound breasts and flour lightly. Melt butter in a foil pan and add garlic; cook chicken in pan over coals until almost done; add remaining ingredients except cornstarch and simmer until chicken is done. Remove chicken and thicken liquid with cornstarch mixed with water. Add chicken to sauce and heat until hot. Serve with rice. Serves 4.

57 CORNISH GAME HENS

All light meat, and stuffed with wild rice!

6, 1 lb Rock Cornish hens
1 T salt
1 T MSG
Basting sauce:
1/2 C soy sauce
1/3 C butter, melted

Stuffing:
1/3 C wild rice blend
2 T soft butter
1/4 C golden raisins
2 T slivered almonds
1/2 t sage
salt to taste

Wash rice and cook in boiling, salted water until tender. Drain and add remaining stuffing ingredients. Thaw frozen hens and season inside of each bird with salt and MSG. Skewer neck skin to back. Fill each bird with 1/4 C stuffing. Insert a flap of foil to close opening. Tie wings to body, and legs to tail with cord. Mount birds either crosswise or lengthwise on spit. Roast with drip pan under birds and with slow coals at back of firebox for 1 hour, or until tender, basting frequently with soy sauce and butter mixture. Serves 6.

58   ROTISSERIE DUCK

A sprinkle of sugar for golden color

1 cleaned duckling, 4 lbs
salt
pepper
2 T sugar

Rub inside of duck with salt. Prick skin and truss well.
Balance duck on spit, securing with holding forks. Arrange
coals at back and sides of firebox and place a foil drip pan
under spit. (Ducks are fat, so it may be necessary to empty
drip pan occasionally to prevent flame up.) Turn on motor
and lower hood. Let duck rotate over medium coals for
about 2 hours or until done. If grill has a heat indicator,
maintain a temperature of 300°. Sprinkle bird with sugar
and pepper about 10 minutes before roasting time is completed. Serves 4.

59 HICKORY SMOKED TURKEY

Dusky-toned meat with a subtle smoke flavor

1 10-12 lb turkey
1/4 C salad oil
1/2 C salt
1 C vinegar
1/4 t pepper
2 t parsley, finely chopped
hickory chips

Rinse bird and pat dry. Make a paste of salad oil and salt;
rub 1/4 cup of paste in both turkey cavities. To remaining
paste, add vinegar, pepper and parsley for basting sauce.
Truss turkey and balance on spit, or use a rotary roast rack.
Brush outside of bird with oil. Place slow coals at back of
firebox, and toss damp hickory chips on coals. Place a foil
drip pan under bird, and a small pan of water at one end of
firebox for moisture. Roast with the hood down. At end of
first hour, baste with sauce. Then, every 30 minutes baste
bird, check coals, hickory and water in pan. Plan on 2 1/2-
3 hours roasting time. About 20 minutes before time is up,
snip cord holding drumsticks. Test for doneness by moving
drumsticks up and down. They should move easily or twist
out of joint. Also press on meat of drumstick; it should feel
very soft. Let finished turkey rest 15 minutes before
carving. Serves 6-8.

MARINADES &
SAUCES

John's Marinade Tips

-For just a flavor accent, you may choose to brush meat before grilling with marinade rather than leaving meat to stand in it for a period of time.

-Quality of meat determines how long to marinate; less tender cuts need to marinate longer.

-Marinate meats submerged in marinade from two hours to overnight in refrigerator.

-Do not put marinades in aluminum containers; use only glass or stainless steel.

60 EASY BASTING SAUCE

Just the right flavor bite

1/2 C catsup	1 T prepared mustard
2 T vinegar	2 t Kitchen Bouquet
2 T honey	dash hot pepper sauce

Combine ingredients and mix well. Use at once or store in refrigerator. Use to baste burgers, steaks, chops or kabobs during broiling. Makes 3/4 cup sauce.

61 CHICKEN BASTING SAUCE

1/4 lb melted butter or margarine
1 T Worcestershire sauce

This mixture will baste a four pound chicken.

62   SOY-BUTTER SAUCE

Basting sauce for game hens

6 T soy sauce
1 T melted butter
1/4 t salt
dash each: pepper, marjoram and MSG

Combine ingredients.

63   NO-COOK BARBEQUE SAUCE

For an oven barbecue too. Good with lamb

1 C mayonnaise	1 T horseradish
3/4 C tomato sauce	1 t salt
1/4 C vinegar	1/2 t pepper
1 T chopped onion	3 T Worcestershire sauce
1/2 t cayenne pepper	1/4-1/2 t hot pepper sauce

Combine all ingredients and blend well. Sauce may be stored for several weeks in refrigerator. Makes 2 cups.

64   SMOKY BARBECUE SAUCE
Bastes four pounds of ribs

1 C tomato sauce	1 t celery seed
1, 4 1/2 oz bottle steak sauce	1/4 t liquid smoke
1/2 C water	

Combine all ingredients. Makes about 2 1/4 cups sauce.

65   SWEET-SOUR SAUCE
Use to baste broiled shrimp, and at the table

1 C sugar	1/2 t salt
1/2 C white vinegar	2 t cornstarch
1/2 C water	1 T cold water
1 T chopped green pepper	1 t paprika
1 T chopped pimiento	

Combine first 5 ingredients and simmer for 5 minutes.
Combine cornstarch with 1 T cold water and add to hot
mixture. Cook and stir until sauce thickens. Cool slightly
and add paprika. Makes 1 1/2 cups sauce.

66   WESTSIDE BARBECUE SAUCE

24 oz Open Pit Barbecue Sauce
1/2 C tomato sauce   1 T garlic powder
2 oz Worcestershire sauce   2 T chili sauce
2 oz steak sauce   1 small onion (optional)
1/2 t lemon juice   1/2 C prepared mustard
2 T vinegar   1 t liquid smoke
salt and pepper

Combine ingredients. If onions are used, boil sauce for 10
minutes. Otherwise, no cooking is necessary.

67 BARBECUE SAUCE

Texas style!

1/2 C vinegar
1 T Worcestershire sauce
1 large onion, diced
2 cloves garlic
1 lemon, juice and peel

1/2 C catsup
1/2 t hot pepper sauce
1 T salt
1/2 t chili powder
dash sage

Grate lemon peel and squeeze the lemon. Put garlic though a press. Combine ingredients and simmer for 15 minutes. Use as a basting sauce, glaze or dip for chicken or ribs.

68 QUICK BORDELAISE SAUCE

Does great things for roast beef

2 carrots, chopped finely
1/4 C butter or margarine
3 T instant minced onion
2/3 C sliced mushrooms

1/3-1/2 C cooking claret
1 1/4 C canned beef gravy
1 T lemon juice
1/2 t MSG

Cook carrots in butter until tender; add onion, mushrooms and claret and simmer uncovered for five minutes. Add beef gravy, lemon juice and MSG. Simmer five minutes more.

69 SAVORY CHICKEN SAUCE

Brush your bird while it broils

1/2 C salad oil
1 1/4 C water
2 T chopped onion
1 clove garlic, crushed
1 1/2 t sugar
1 t salt
1 t chili powder

1 t paprika
1 t pepper
1/2 t dry mustard
dash cayenne pepper
2 T vinegar
1 t Worcestershire sauce
1 t hot pepper sauce

Combine and simmer ingredients for 30 minutes.

70 PEPPY SEAFOOD SAUCE

Serve with shrimp

1/3 C chili sauce
2 T lemon juice
1 T horseradish
1 t Worcestershire sauce
2 drops hot pepper sauce

Combine and chill. 1/2 cup sauce.

71   ROSEMARY MARINADE

For chicken or lamb

1/4 C salad oil	2 t crushed rosemary
1/4 C vinegar	1/2 t pepper
2 t salt	1/2 C sliced onion

Combine ingredients and marinate chicken or lamb from 1 hour to overnight.

72   TENDER-UP BEEF MARINADE

Add spicy flavor while rump roast tenderizes

2 1/2 C vinegar	12 whole cloves
2 1/2 C water	2-3 bay leaves
3 onions, sliced	6 black peppercorns
1 lemon, sliced	1 1/2 T salt

Combine ingredients and let stand at room temperature for 24 hours, then add meat. For mild flavor, marinate in refrigerator 24 hours; for more tenderizing and flavor, refrigerate in marinade 2-3 days before cooking.

73 ARMENIAN HERB MARINADE

For chicken or lamb

1/2 C olive oil or salad oil
1/4 C lemon juice
1 t salt
1 t marjoram
1 t thyme

1/2 t pepper
1 clove garlic, minced
1/2 C chopped onion
1/4 C snipped parsley

Combine ingredients and marinate chicken or lamb from 1 hour to overnight.

74 TERIYAKI MARINADE

For lamb and tender beef

2/3 C soy sauce
1/4 C salad oil
6 cloves garlic, minced
2 t MSG

2 t ginger <u>or</u>
2 T grated gingerroot
2 t dry mustard
2 T molasses

Combine all ingredients in a glass bowl and let stand at room temperature for 24 hours. Marinate meat from 1 hour to overnight. Enough marinade for two pounds of meat.

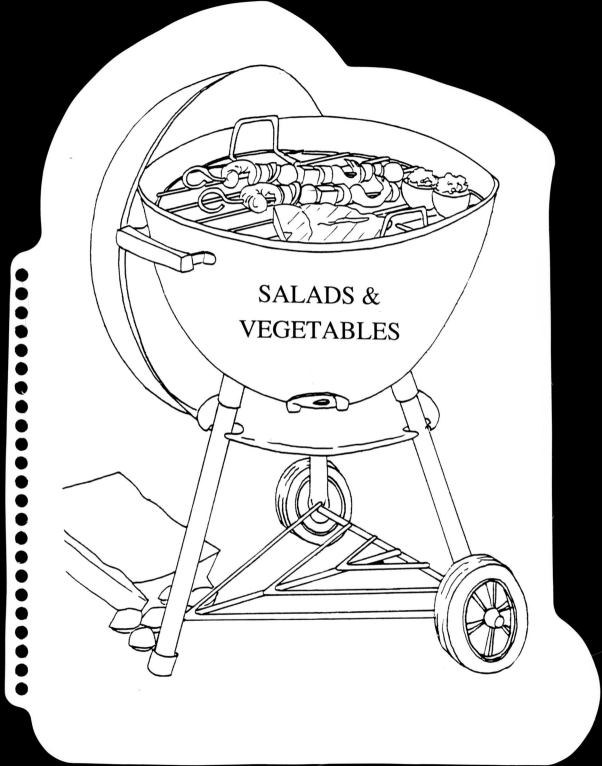

SALADS &
VEGETABLES

75 GARDEN PLATTER SALAD

Dutch onion rings make this special

Dutch onion rings:
2 medium sweet onions
1/4 C dairy sour cream
1/4 t salt
1/2 t celery seed
1 t lemon juice

2-3 large tomatoes
1 small cucumber
Italian salad dressing
1/4 t salt
1/4 t coarse black pepper
1/2 t dill seed
1 t snipped fresh parsley

Slice onions 1/4 inch thick; separate into rings and cover with boiling water. Let stand 2 minutes and drain. Chill onions. Before serving, combine sour cream, salt, celery seed and lemon juice; toss with onions. Slice tomatoes and cucumbers. Pile onions in center of a platter and border these with overlapping slices of tomatoes and cucumbers; drizzle Italian dressing over slices, then sprinkle with salt, pepper, dill seed and parsley. Garnish platter with ripe olives and leaf lettuce if desired. 6-8 servings.

76 ITALIAN SALAD BOWL

1/2 medium head lettuce
1/2 medium head romaine
2 C sliced, raw zucchini
1/2 C sliced mushrooms
1/2 C sliced radishes

3 green onions
salt and pepper
Italian or wine vinegar
   dressing
1/2 C crumbled blue cheese

Tear lettuce and romaine in bite-sized pieces; combine in a large salad bowl with other vegetables. Season to taste and toss lightly with dressing. Sprinkle with blue cheese. Serves 6.

77 WILTED SPINACH SALAD

Simply delicious!

1 lb fresh spinach
4 green onions
coarse black pepper
6-8 slices bacon, diced
1/4 C wine vinegar

2 T sugar
1/2 t salt
1/2 lb sliced mushrooms
4 hard-boiled eggs

Wash spinach, discard stems and pat dry; tear into bite-sized pieces and place in salad bowl. Slice onions with tops and slice mushrooms; add to spinach. Grind pepper over vegetables. Just before serving, fry bacon bits; add vinegar, sugar and salt to bacon and drippings. Pour hot mixture over spinach and toss until coated and slightly wilted. Sprinkle with chopped eggs. Serves 4-6.

78   SPRING SALAD BOWL

Make dressing a few hours ahead

Dressing:
1 1/3 C salad oil
1/2 C vinegar
1 1/2 t salt
1 t sugar
1/2 t dry mustard
4 cloves garlic

1/2 head lettuce
1 C sliced celery
1 C sliced radishes
1/2 small head cauliflower
1/2 t salt
1/3 C (2 oz) blue cheese

Peel and cut garlic cloves in half; combine with remaining dressing ingredients, cover, shake well and refrigerate for several hours. Break lettuce into bite-sized pieces; add celery, radishes, sliced cauliflower and salt. Sprinkle with crumbled cheese. Shake dressing well, remove garlic and toss salad with enough dressing to coat leaves. Serve immediately. Serves 6-8.

79 BACON LETTUCE & TOMATO SALAD

A country club favorite

romaine lettuce leaves
1/2 head lettuce
3 ripe tomatoes
1 C croutons

8 slices bacon
1/2 C mayonnaise
salt and pepper

Cook bacon until crisp; drain and crumble. Line salad bowl with romaine. Break head lettuce into bite-sized pieces. Cut tomatoes into wedges and add with bacon to head lettuce. Add mayonnaise and toss lightly; season to taste with salt and pepper and pile in salad bowl.
Serves 4-6.

To make your own croutons, toast bread cubes in slow oven, 225° until dry, about 2 hours.

80 CAESAR SALAD

A hearty main dish or a barbecue go-with

1 clove garlic
1/2 C salad oil
2-3 slices white bread
Parmesan cheese
1/2 head lettuce
1/2 bunch curly endive
1, 2 oz can anchovies

3-4 tomatoes, diced
1 beaten egg
1/2 C Parmesan cheese
1/4 C lemon juice
1 t Worcestershire sauce
1/2 t pepper
1/2 t salt

Mash garlic and add to salad oil; let stand. Cut bread in cubes, spread on a baking sheet, pour a little of the garlic oil over them and bake at 225°, for 2 hours. Sprinkle with Parmesan cheese. Break lettuce and endive into salad bowl and add croutons, anchovies and tomatoes. Strain salad oil to remove garlic and pour over vegetables. Combine remaining ingredients for dressing and beat well. Pour dressing over salad and toss lightly. Serves 6.

81 POTATO SALAD SPECIAL

Its terrific! Cauliflower slices and bacon dressing

3 C diced, cooked potatoes   6 slices bacon
1 1/2 C raw cauliflower   1 C mayonnaise
1 C diced celery   1 T bacon fat
2 hard-cooked eggs   2 t caraway seed (optional)
1/4 C chopped onion   salt

Slice cauliflower and add to potatoes, celery, chopped eggs
and onion. Fry bacon until crisp; crumble and add to
vegetables. Combine mayonnaise with bacon fat and
caraway seed; pour over salad and toss lightly.
Salt to taste. Serves 4-6.

82 HOT GERMAN POTATO SALAD

A sweet-sour salad for a barbecue

1/2 lb bacon	dash pepper
1/2 C chopped onion	1/2 C vinegar
2 T flour	1 C water
1 1/2 t salt	6 large, cooked potatoes
1 t celery seed	2 T snipped parsley

Cook bacon until crisp; drain and crumble, reserving 1/4 cup fat. Cook onion in reserved fat until tender, but not brown. Blend in flour, sugar, salt, celery seed and pepper. Add vinegar and water; cook and stir until mixture thickens. Slice potatoes, add bacon and pour hot dressing over potatoes; mix lightly, sprinkle with parsley and serve warm. Serves 6-8.

83   OLD-FASHIONED COLESLAW

A dandy compliment to barbecued meat

2/3 C evaporated milk
2 T sugar
1/2 t pepper
2-3 T vinegar
3 C finely shredded cabbage

Combine milk, sugar, salt and pepper, stirring briskly. Add
vinegar slowly to suit taste. Chill. (Mixture will thicken.)
Rinse shredded cabbage in slightly warm water and drain
well; cover and chill 1 hour or more. Toss cabbage with
dressing. Serves 4.

84 FRESH FRUIT SALAD

1 6 oz can concentrated
  orange juice
1 can water
1/4 medium watermelon
1/2 cantaloupe
1/2 honeydew melon
2 apples

1 C sweet cherries
2 bananas
2 oranges
2 peaches
2 pears
1 C green grapes
1 C red grapes

Dice, slice, or use a melon baller to cut fruit in bite-sized pieces. Combine all ingredients and garnish with mint leaves. Serves 6-8.

85 PEPPERONI SALAD

Strictly Italian

1 head lettuce	1/2 C sliced pepperoni
2 tomatoes	1/4 C sliced green onion
4 oz Mozzarella cheese	1/2 C Italian dressing
1 C garbanzo beans	salt and pepper

Break lettuce into bite-sized pieces. Cut cheese in cubes.
Cut tomatoes in wedges. Combine all ingredients and toss
lightly. Season to taste. Chill. Serves 6-8.

86 HICKORY SMOKED EARS

Smoky flavor penetrates each kernel

Turn back husks of fresh corn and strip off corn silk. Lay
husks back in position and place ears on grill over hot
coals. Add damp hickory to coals, lower hood and cook for
about 1 hour.

87 GOURMET GRILLED CORN

Elegant corn-on-the-cob

8 ears sweet corn
1/2 C cashew nut spread or creamy peanut butter
8 slices bacon

Turn back corn husks and strip off silk. Spread each ear
with 1 tablespoon of nut spread. Spiral a slice of bacon
around each ear. Lay husks back in position and place over
hot coals. Turn frequently until done, about 20 minutes.
 8 servings.

88 FRESH CORN ON THE COB

Pass horseradish, anise, or herb flavored butter

Remove husks and silk from fresh corn. Place each ear on
a piece of foil, spread with soft butter, and sprinkle with
salt and pepper. Wrap foil around ear, but do not seal.
(The corn will roast, rather than steam.) Roast directly over
hot coals 15-20 minutes, or until corn is tender, turning ears
frequently. Offer extra butter and seasonings.

89 GOLDEN CORN FRY

Leftover ears? Try this!

2 T butter	1 clove garlic
3 C cut corn	salt and pepper
1/2 C light cream	1/4 C Parmesan cheese
2 T chopped chives	

Fold a 3 foot length of 18 inch foil in half. Form a pouch in
foil and add all ingredients except cheese. Fold foil tightly
and place on grill. Heat for 10-15 minutes. Open package
and sprinkle with cheese. Let stand on side of grill until
cheese melts. 4-6 Servings.

90 CHEEZY BACON POTATOES

One package feeds a family; and such flavor!

3 large baking potatoes
salt and pepper
4-5 slices bacon, fried and drained
1 large onion, sliced
6 T Parmesan cheese
1/4 C butter or margarine

Slice potatoes onto a large piece of foil and sprinkle with salt and pepper. Crumble bacon over potatoes, pile on cheese cubes and onion slices. Slice cold butter over all. Bring edges of foil up and seal, leaving a little space for steam expansion. Seal well with a double fold. Place package on grill and cook over coals for about one hour turning severa! times, or cook on grill with barbecue hood down for about 45 minutes. Serves 4.

91 ONION HERBED POTATOES

Add your choice of cheese on tops of baked potatoes

8 medium baking potatoes
1/2 C melted margarine
1 envelope onion soup mix
2 t dried parsley
1 1/2 t seasoned salt

Wash and cut potatoes in quarters lengthwise. Cut 8
squares foil large enough to wrap potatoes. Dry potatoes
and place each one on foil; mix remaining ingredients and
spoon over cut sides of potatoes. Pull sides of foil together,
fold over twice, leaving room for steam expansion. Fold in
ends of foil toward potato. Place on grill above medium
coals and cook 35-45 minutes. Potatoes are done when
they are slightly soft. Open foil, add cheese if desired and
serve. 8 Servings.

92 PEAS AND MUSHROOMS

A favorite combination

1, 10 oz pkg frozen peas
salt and pepper
3 T butter or margarine
1, 3 oz can broiled, sliced mushrooms

Place block of frozen peas on a large square of foil. Season with salt and pepper and top with butter and drained mushrooms. Bring edges of foil up and leaving a little space for expansion, seal tightly with a double fold. Place package over hot coals for about 10-15 minutes. Turn occasionally. 4 servings.

93 HERB-STUFFED MUSHROOMS

A mushroom lover's treat

12 large, fresh mushrooms
1/3 C sauterne wine
1 beef bouillon cube
1/2 t MSG

2 T finely chopped onion
2 T butter or margarine
1/4 C herb-seasoned stuffing

Remove stems from mushrooms and reserve. In a saucepan, combine sauterne, bouillon cube and MSG; heat until
cube dissolves. Add mushroom caps, tops down, and
simmer 2-3 minutes. Chop mushroom stems and cook with
onion in butter until tender. Stir in stuffing mix and 2
tablespoons of wine mixture. Fit two mushroom caps
together with about 1 tablespoon of filling. String on
skewers. Turn skewers over hot coals 2-3 minutes, brushing occasionally with melted butter. (Double filling recipe
for very large mushrooms.) 6 double mushrooms.
Serves 3 or 6.

94   RICE WITH MUSHROOMS

Good with steak, lamb chops or hamburgers

1 1/3 C minute rice
1 3 oz can mushrooms
1 C cold water
1/4 C finely chopped onion

1 t Worcestershire sauce
1/2 t salt
2 T butter

Fold a 3 foot length of 18 inch foil in half. Form a pouch in the foil, and add rice, mushrooms with liquid, water, onion and seasoning. Stir to mix and dot with butter. Fold edges of foil and seal tightly. Place on grill over hot coals and heat 15-18 minutes. Before serving, open foil, add a pat of butter and fluff rice with a fork. 4 servings.

95 CHEESE TOPPED TOMATOES

As pretty as they are delicious

5 large ripe tomatoes
salt and pepper
1/4 C soft bread crumbs
1/4 C shredded sharp cheese
1 T butter, melted
snipped parsley

Slice off tops of tomatoes making zig-zag edges. Season
with salt and pepper. Combine bread crumbs and cheese
and add melted butter; sprinkle mixture evenly over
tomatoes. Garnish with parsley. Heat tomatoes on a sheet
of foil over coals until warm and cheese is melted.
Serve immediately. 5 servings.

96 HOBO RICE

Fun to cook on the grill; the fluffiest rice ever!

1/2 C water
1/2 t salt
1/2 C minute rice

Combine water and salt in a 1 lb coffee can. Heat to
boiling over hot coals. Remove from heat and add rice; stir
just to moisten. Cover can tightly with foil and set at grill
side, <u>away</u> from heat. Let stand for 13 minutes. 3 cups
rice. Serves 4-6.

97 CHINESE FRIED RICE

Perfect with teriyaki or barbecued roast

1 1/3 C minute rice
1/4 C salad oil
1 onion, minced
2 eggs
soy sauce

Cook rice is a heavy pan according to package directions.
In a skillet, heat oil and cook onion until tender, but not
brown. Add eggs and scramble with onions; add rice
before eggs set and mix well. Add soy sauce to taste.
4-6 servings.

98   ZUCCHINI PARMESAN

Fine summer squash, prepared without tomato

6 C thinly sliced zucchini	2 T butter
1 small onion, sliced	salt and pepper
1 T water	3 T Parmesan cheese

Put all ingredients except cheese in a skillet; cook uncovered for approximately 5 minutes, until barely tender, turning occasionally with a spatula. Sprinkle with cheese and serve. Serves 8.

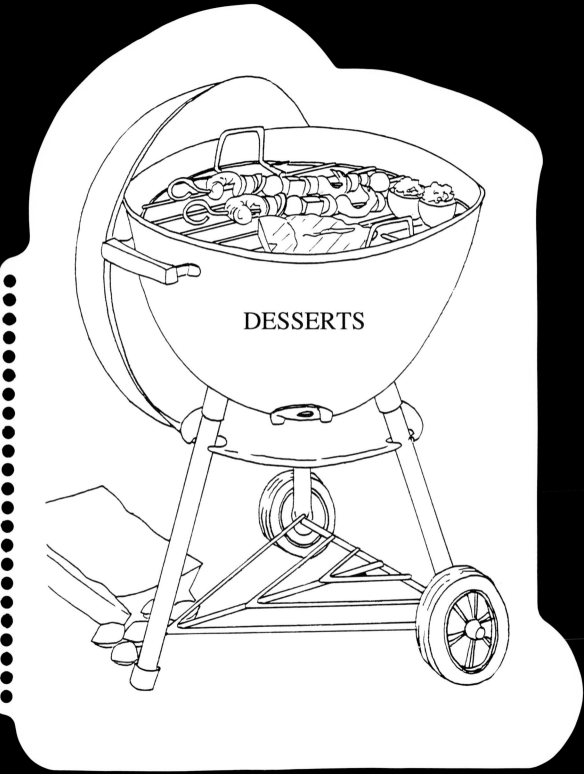

DESSERTS

DESSERTS

DESSERTS

99 HOT BANANA SHORTCAKE

Bananas Foster barbecue style

1/4 C butter or margarine
2-3 green tipped bananas
2 T lemon juice
2/3 C brown sugar

1/4 t cinnamon
4 1-inch slices pound cake or
   angel food loaf cake
vanilla ice cream or
   sour cream

Heat butter in a foilware pan over hot coals. Peel and slice bananas; add to butter. Drizzle lemon juice over bananas and sprinkle with brown sugar and cinnamon. Cook until bananas are just soft, spooning the syrup over occasionally. Toast pound cake slices on both sides on grill. To serve, place toasted cake slices on plates and spoon bananas and syrup over them. Top with ice cream or sour cream. Serves 4.

100 HOMEMADE ICE CREAM

Was there ever a better dessert?

Basic recipe:

1 1/2 C sugar	2 eggs, slightly beaten
1 envelope unflavored gelatin	2 t vanilla
8 C half and half	1/2 t salt

Combine sugar and gelatin in a saucepan. Add 4 C half
and half, and stir over low heat until gelatin dissolves. Stir
a small amount of hot mixture into eggs and then return
eggs to hot mixture; cook until thickened slightly. Chill.
Add remaining half and half, vanilla and salt. 3 quarts ice
cream.

To freeze ice cream: Pour chilled mixture into freezer can,
filling only 2/3 full to allow for expansion. Fit can into
freezer and attach dasher and cover. Pack crushed ice and
coarse ice cream (rock salt) around can, using 6 parts ice to
1 part salt. Pack ice up to, but not over cover. Turn crank
until it becomes difficult to turn or follow freezer directions

if using an electric freezer, adding more ice and salt as needed to maintain ice level. Flavor improves if ice cream stands to ripen. Remove dasher, replace lid and plug hole in lid. Cover can with more ice and salt, and cover the freezer with a rug. Let stand for about 4 hours.

Variations:

Strawberry: Decrease sugar to 1 cup in basic mixture. Crush 1 quart fresh, ripe strawberries with 3/4 C sugar and add to chilled mixture.

Peach: Decrease sugar to 1 cup in basic mixture. Combine 2 cups mashed peaches, 3/4 C sugar and 1/4 t almond extract and add to chilled mixture.

Maraschino cherry: Add 1/3 cup maraschino cherries and 1 tablespoon cherry juice to chilled mixture.

Chocolate Almond: Increase sugar in basic mixture to 2 cups. To sugar-gelatin mixture add 2 cups semi-sweet chocolate pieces, and proceed as directed. To chilled mixture add 3/4 C toasted, slivered almonds.

101   CHOCOLATE CHIP CHUNKS

1/4 C brown sugar

1/4 C white sugar

1/3 C margarine

1 large egg

2 C flour

1 C chocolate chips

1 t vanilla

Cream sugars and margarine; add egg and blend. Stir in flour, chocolate chips and vanilla. Prepare a 12 inch square foil pan with 3 layers of foil. Spray inside with non-stick spray. Form dough into 24 small balls and place in pan; do not flatten. Bake in a medium hot covered grill, 12-15 minutes. Serve with homemade ice cream.

102   HOMEMADE HOT FUDGE SAUCE

1/2 lb chocolate (type used for making candy)

black coffee

Melt the chocolate in a small sauce pan at side of grill away from the fire, stirring occasionally. Add enough black coffee to thin it to ice cream sauce consistency. If chocolate thickens, add more coffee.

103 HOT CAKES

Little hot dessert cakes

Cut a pound cake or angel food cake into 1 1/2 inch cubes.
Spear each cube on a fork and dip in melted currant jelly,
sweetened condensed milk, or a mixture of 1/2 cup honey
and 1 tablespoon lemon juice. Then roll the cube in flaked
coconut to cover. String cubes on skewers and toast over
very hot coals, turning often. Serves 6-8.

104 DONUT HOLES

Spectacular on a small scale

Cut a tube of refrigerated biscuits into thirds, and roll each
piece in a ball. String balls on skewers, leaving 1/2 inch
between each one. "Bake" over hot coals, turning constantly, until browned and completely done, about 7
minutes. At once, push balls off skewers into melted
butter, then roll in cinnamon sugar mixture. One tube of
biscuits makes 30 pieces. Serves 6-8.

105   OUTDOOR APPLE DUMPLINGS

Combine 2 cans apple pie filling and 2/3 cup water in a
large skillet with a tight-fitting cover. Place on hot grill (or
kitchen range.) When apples come to a boil, cut one tube
of refrigerated biscuits in quarters and let the pieces drop
onto the bubbling apples. Sprinkle biscuits with cinnamon-
sugar. Cover and let simmer 20 minutes. Serve with
cream. Serves 6-8.

106 FRESH FRUIT ON A SPIT

Fresh fruit with a different flavor

1 fresh pineapple   2 dozen large strawberries
1 cantaloupe   4 fresh peaches
6 kiwi fruit

Peel and cut fruit into 1 inch cubes. String on 2 spits or on skewers ending each one with a berry. Place over medium coals 3-4 minutes. Sprinkle with powdered sugar and serve while warm.

107 FRUIT KABOBS

A delightful dessert with ice cream

1 tube refrigerated
   cinnamon rolls
2 dozen maraschino cherries
1 can pineapple chunks

2 dozen marshmallows
4 medium bananas

Open and place cinnamon rolls in a buttered foil pan; place pan on a medium grill with cover down. When rolls are done, cool slightly and cut in quarters. Open and drain cherries and pineapple. Peel and cut bananas in 1 inch pieces. Dip the pieces of banana into pineapple juice. Alternate the five items on 6, 8 inch skewers, ending with cherries. Let your guests roast them over medium hot coals and eat them immediately. Serves 8.

John Farris has more than 25 years experience preparing foods, both plain and fancy. He has traveled widely to increase his knowledge of several cuisines, and has used this knowledge in his classrooms, teaching future chefs their craft. Restaurants, clubs, hotels, military establishments and universitites have benefited from his advice and expertise. John is a member of the American Culinary Federation, and the Capitol Professional Chef's and Cook's Association of Lansing, Michigan, where he makes his home.

The Grand Cookbook Series